A First Book of
BEETHOVEN

A First Book of
BEETHOVEN

FOR THE BEGINNING PIANIST with DOWNLOADABLE MP3s

Edited by
David Dutkanicz

DOVER PUBLICATIONS, INC.
Mineola, New York

All songs available as downloadable MP3s!

Go to: http://www.doverpublications.com/0486452859
to access these files.

Bibliographical Note

A First Book of Beethoven is a new work, first published by Dover Publications, Inc., in 2004.
The editor would like to thank David Vincola of DV8 Music for his help in preparing the score.

International Standard Book Number

ISBN-13: 978-0-486-45285-2
ISBN-10: 0-486-45285-9

Manufactured in the United States by LSC Communications
45285916   2020
www.doverpublications.com

Contents

Editor's Note

Continuing Dover's renowned series, *A First Book of Beethoven* is meant to bring the joys of Beethoven's music to beginning pianists of all ages. These carefully selected and arranged pieces are designed to develop both the fingers and ears, as well as introduce the more memorable masterpieces of the composer. Most of the works focus on a specific skill: e.g., reading notes above the staff in *Rondo* beginning on page 9, and double-octaves in the *Piano Concerto No. 4* on page 34. Fingerings are provided as a suggestion and should not be taken too literally, as each set of hands playing these arrangements is unique. Teachers and students will be the best judges of that. Also, phrasing and pedaling are left open so as to make the music less daunting. These too can be filled in as the student progresses.

Romance in F

This charming *Romance* was originally written for violin and piano. Be careful of the sharps and flats, and don't rush. The tempo is marked *Andante,* which means "at a walking pace."

Andante

Sonata No. 14

2nd Movement (opening)

All together, Beethoven wrote 32 sonatas for piano. This stately theme is from the opening of the second movement of the fourteenth sonata. Play it gracefully, and be sure to give the notes with sharps an extra push.

Allegretto

Symphony No. 8

(opening)

The Eighth Symphony is considered to be one of Beethoven's lighter and happier works. It was first performed in 1814, and recalls the classical flavors of earlier music. The famous French composer Hector Berlioz said that this melody "fell straight from heaven."

Canto Pastoral

A *pastoral* is a musical work meant to invoke the peace and calmness of the countryside. Taken from Beethoven's nature-themed Symphony No. 6, the simple melody mimics a shepherd's horn, calling his flock home at sunset.

Allegretto

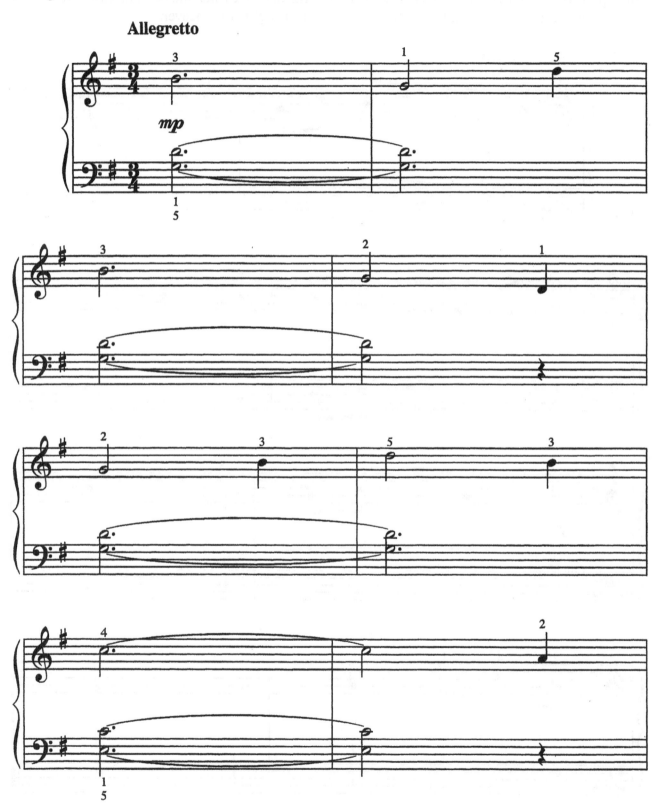

Ode to Joy

This famous melody is the theme of the last movement of Beethoven's Symphony No. 9. For this special symphony, Beethoven included a huge chorus to sing along with the orchestra. The words are taken from a poem by Friedrich Schiller: *Joy, we are under your divine spell. All men become brothers wherever joy is found…*

Steady and March-like

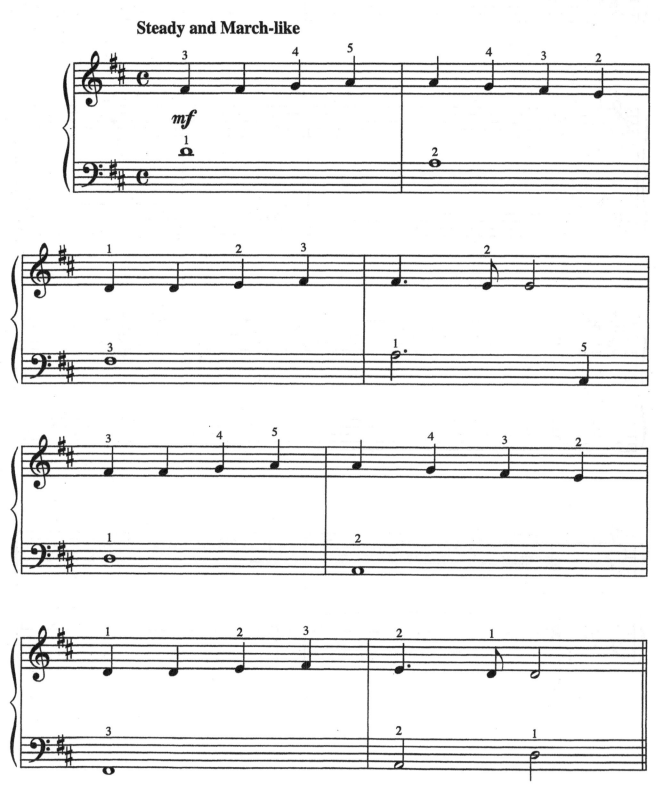

Minuet in G

This delightful court dance is one of Beethoven's most famous. Despite his reputation as a very serious composer, he was fond of writing short dance music. A *minuet* is written in triple meter and accented on the first beat, much like a waltz.

Andantino

Rondo

A sad melody taken from one of Beethoven's lesser known works, *Sonatine*, it climbs high up the piano. Be sure to play it smoothly, and follow the dynamics closely so that you can create a contrast between the different sections.

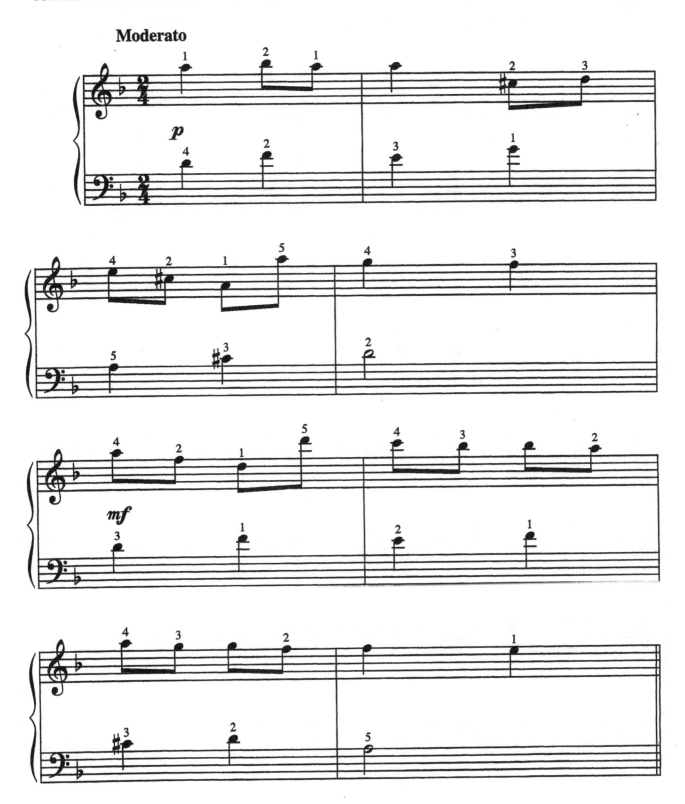

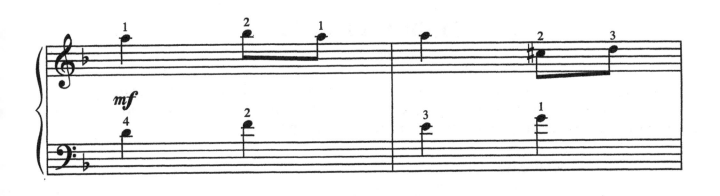

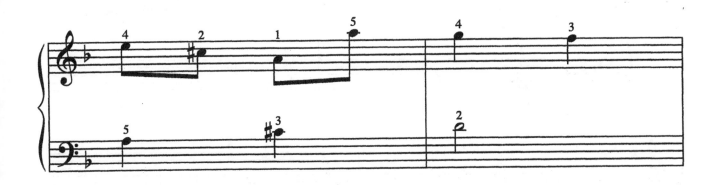

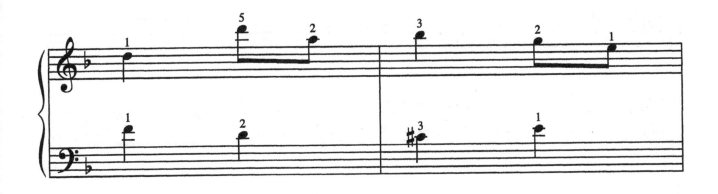

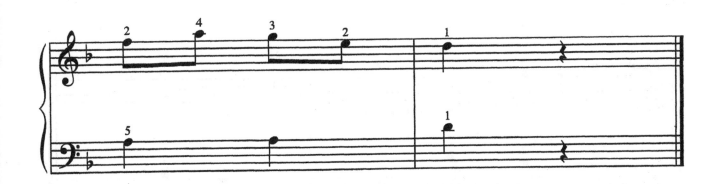

Sonatina in G

(opening)

A *sonatina* is a shorter version of a *sonata*, and usually has two brief movements as opposed to three longer ones. This endearing work was composed around 1785, when **Beethoven** was a teenager. And ever since then, it's been a favorite amongst pianists.

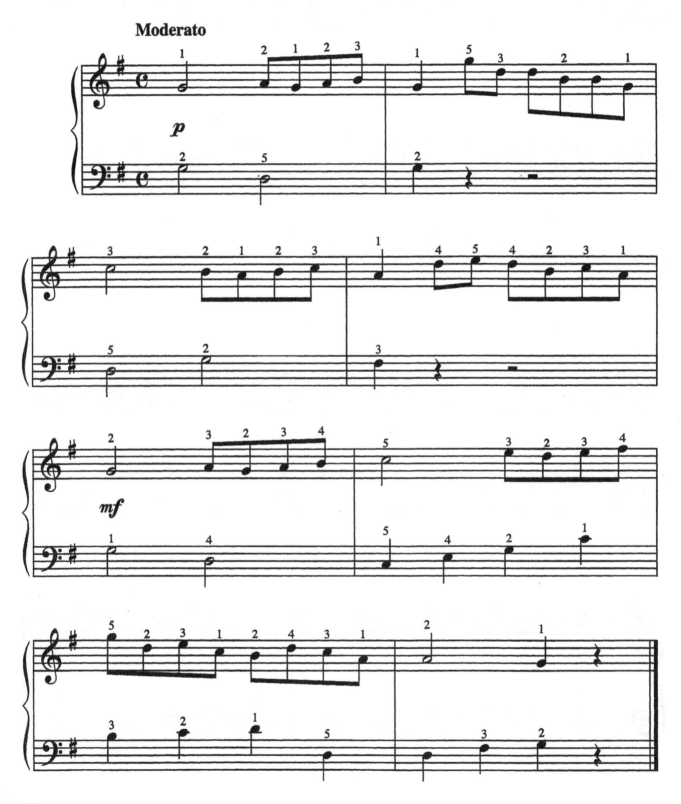

Romanza

This *romanza* is the second movement of the *Sonatina in G* found on the previous page. As with all *romanzas*, it should be played gently and tenderly, and not too fast. An *allegretto* is played slightly slower than *allegro*.

Allegretto

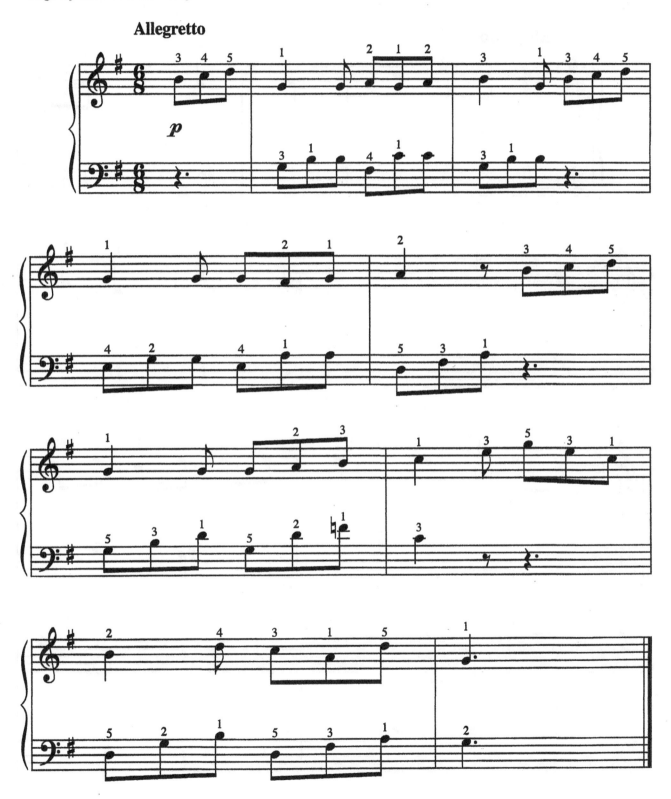

Bagatelle in G Minor

Bagatelle in Italian means "a trifle." Composers would use this label on shorter compositions they felt were more for personal amusement and entertainment. Remember, there were no stereo systems during the time of Beethoven and music had to be played on a keyboard in the home to be heard.

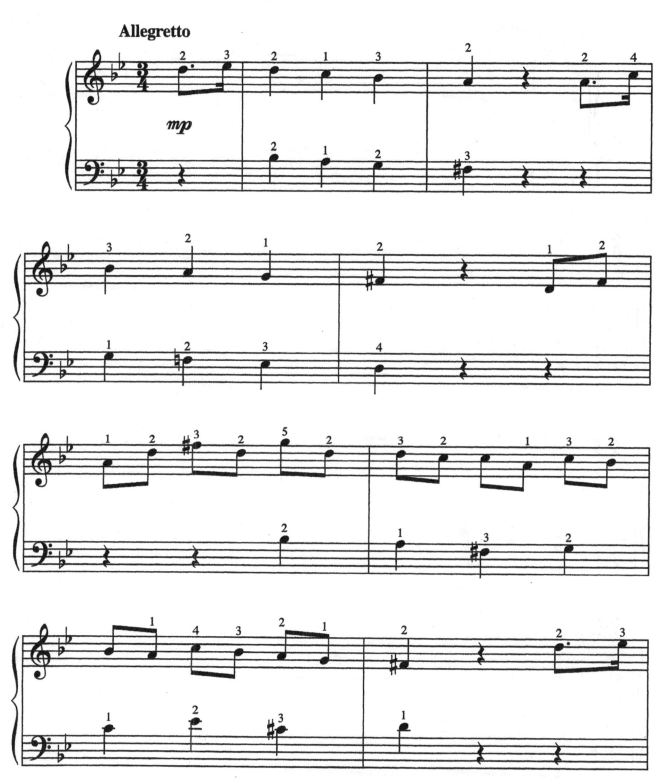

Symphony No. 3

(Theme)

Symphony No. 3 is nicknamed the "Eroica." It was written to honor "heroes" and was originally dedicated to Napoleon Bonaparte. Play the melody in a crisp manner, as if it were a military march.

Allegretto

Adagio

This *adagio* is taken from Beethoven's Sonata No. 5 for piano. Notice the *crescendo* (*cresc.*) on the third line. Be sure to gradually get louder as the melody goes up until you reach a *mezzo forte* (*mf*) at the top.

Bagatelle in D

Another of Beethoven's *bagatelles*, this piece includes wide leaps in the melody. There's no need to fret or overextend your hand. Prepare for the leaps by having the next finger ready and lifting your wrist as you move your arm over to play the note.

Moderato

Rondo

This theme is taken from the opening of the second movement of Beethoven's Sonata No. 19 for piano. The melody is a bit wavy; shape the phrases and follow their ups and downs.

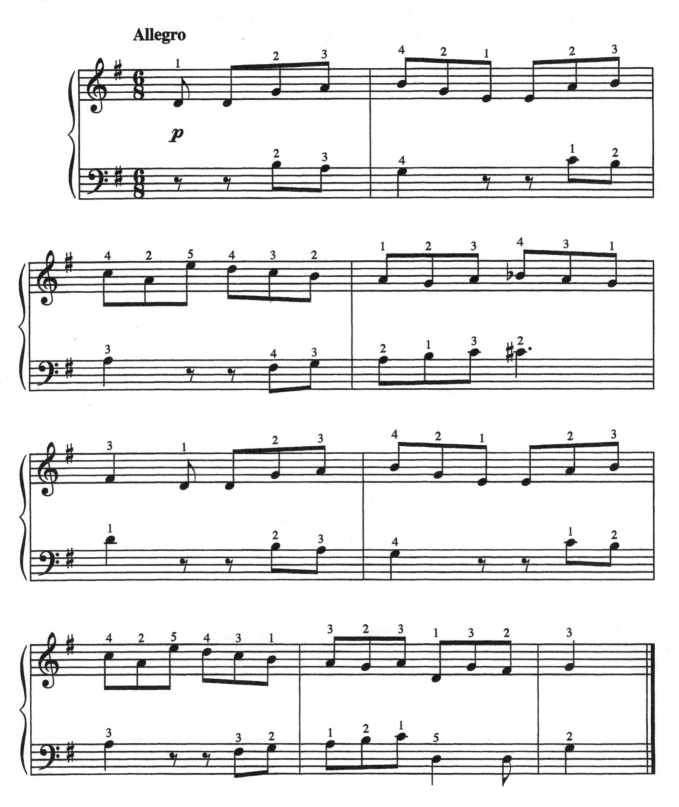

Moonlight Sonata
(opening)

This famous music is taken from the opening of Piano Sonata No. 14. Over the years it has gained the nickname "Moonlight." Play it in a slow manner, and once you are comfortable with the notes, add a sustained effect by applying the right pedal with your foot.

Adagio

Trio

Taken from Sonata No.1 for piano, this *trio* is the middle melody of the third movement. Notice the slurs, they can be tricky. The notes are grouped together in sets of three, in both the right and left hands.

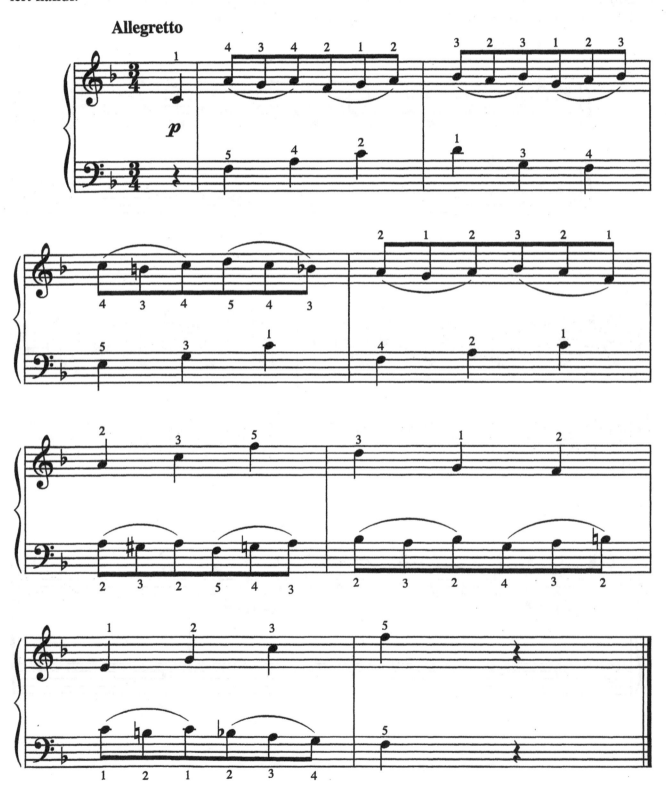

Bagatelle in G

In this piece, pay special attention to the rhythm. Notice the ties–these notes are held and not struck again. In the left hand, bring out the notes that rhythmically echo the right.

Moderato

Symphony No. 5

(opening)

This is the most famous of all of Beethoven's compositions, if not of all music. It was premiered in 1808 at an all-Beethoven concert, with Beethoven himself conducting. Note that the melody (e.g. measure 5) begins in the right hand and continues into the left–try to make it as smooth as possible.

Allegro con brio

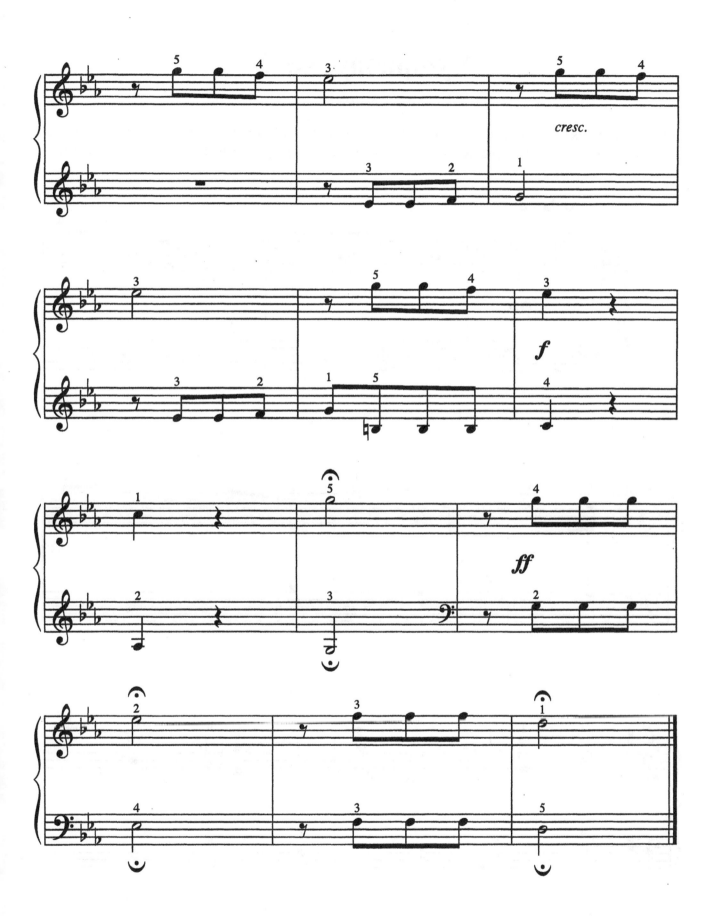

Symphony No. 5

2nd Movement

Although not as famous as the opening, the second movement of Beethoven's Symphony No. 5 is a masterpiece. It should be played evenly, and with less intensity to contrast the first movement.

Symphony No. 6

(opening)

Beethoven was very fond of the countryside, and it was in nature that he found most of his inspiration. Symphony No. 6 is a program piece depicting a day in the country. This opening movement is subtitled: *Awakening of joyous feelings upon arrival in the country.*

Allegro ma non troppo

Adagio Cantabile

This famous piece is the opening to the second movement of the Piano Sonata No. 8, which is also known as the "Pathétique." The melody in the right hand should be played gently, while the left hand should be kept as even as possible. Be sure not to overshadow or overpower the melody

Turkish March

In Beethoven's times, Turkish culture was considered exotic and became popular. Musically, composers would adopt such Turkish instruments as cymbals and use them in marches for an effect. When you play this march, try to hear cymbals clanging in the background.

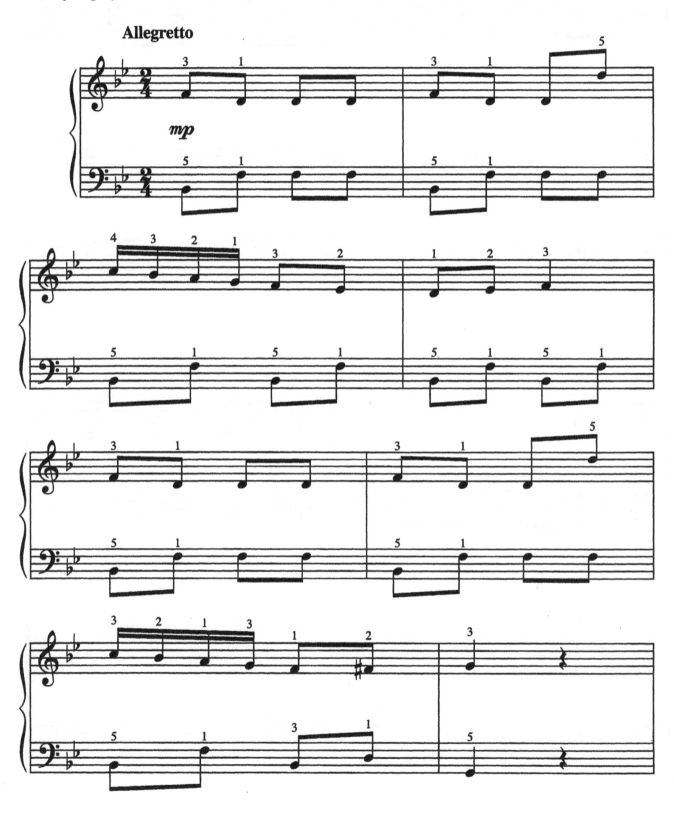

Piano Concerto No. 4

2nd Movement

Not only was Beethoven a composer, he was also a virtuoso pianist who premiered his own concertos. This particular concerto calls for extreme contrast, with the opening played loudly by the orchestra and then softly soothed by the piano.

Andante

Für Elise

This famous work was written around 1810. It is thought that Beethoven wrote it to a lost love. Connect the notes in the left hand with those in the right as smoothly as possible to keep the music beautifully flowing.

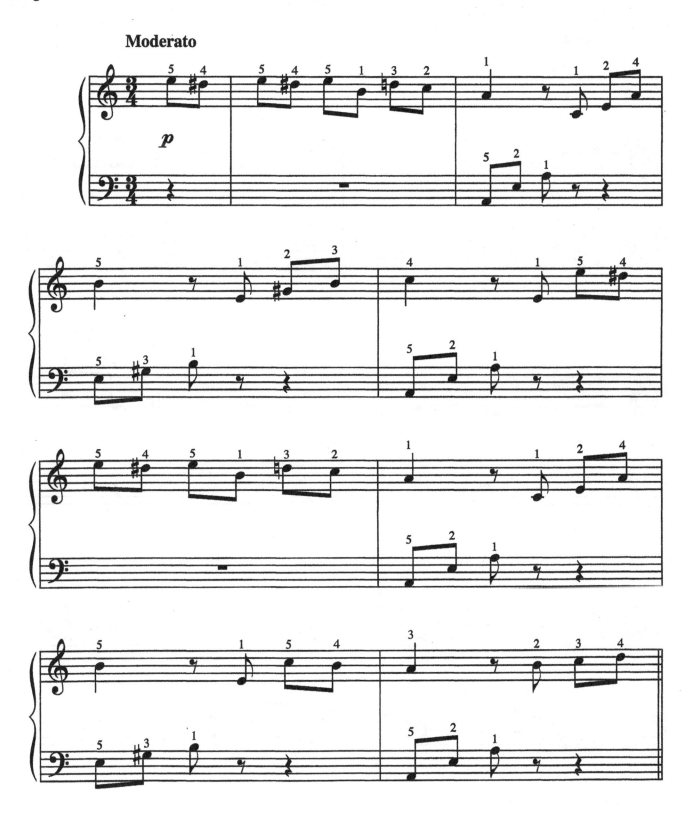

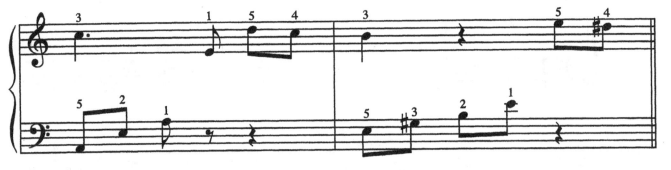

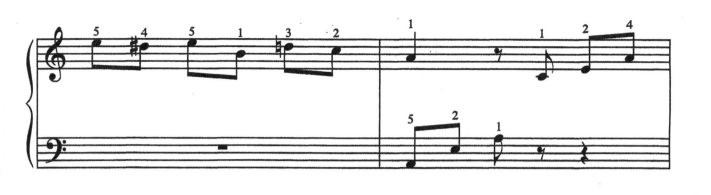